MASTER THE UKULELE 1

BY TERRY CARTER

UKE LIKE THE PROS

ISBN-13: 978-0-9826151-6-4

UKELIKETHEPROS.COM

C O N T E N T S

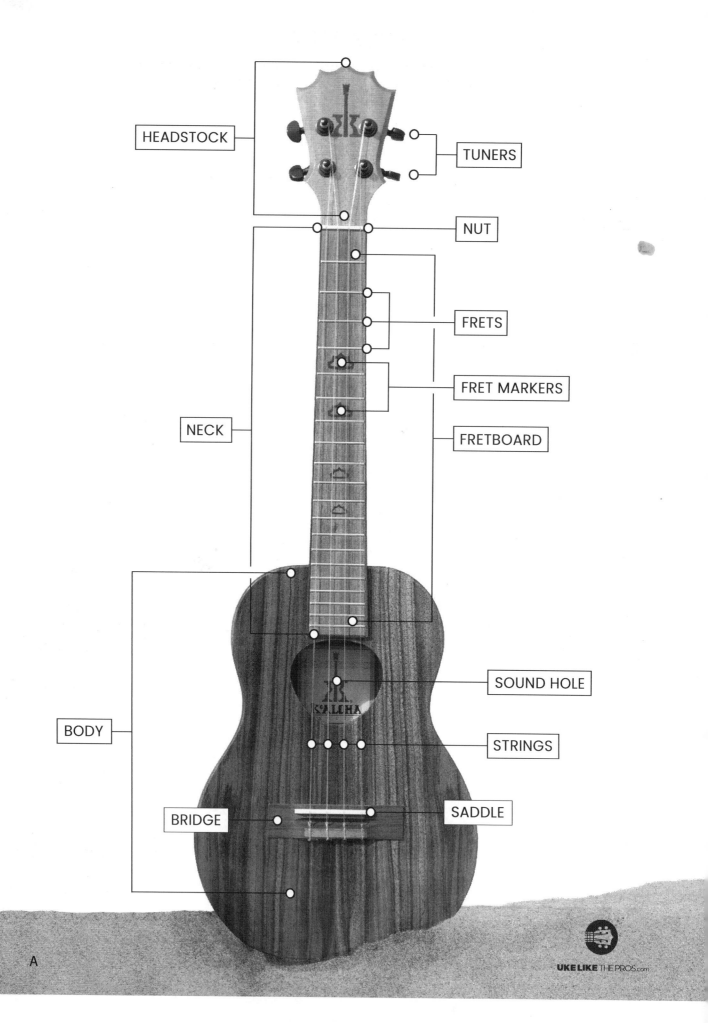

HEADSTOCK

TUNERS

NUT

FRETS

FRET MARKERS

FRETBOARD

NECK

SOUND HOLE

BODY

STRINGS

BRIDGE

SADDLE

A

THE ESSENTIALS

It is important to learn and memorize these terms and symbols because they not only apply to Ukulele but to all music.

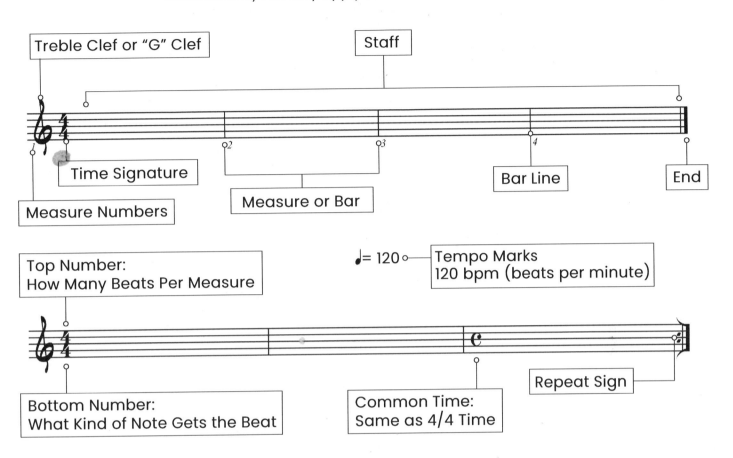

Treble Clef or "G" Clef · **Staff** · **Time Signature** · **Measure Numbers** · **Measure or Bar** · **Bar Line** · **End**

Top Number:
How Many Beats Per Measure

♩ = 120 — **Tempo Marks**
120 bpm (beats per minute)

Bottom Number:
What Kind of Note Gets the Beat

Common Time:
Same as 4/4 Time

Repeat Sign

Notes On The Staff: There are seven notes in music (A, B, C, D, E, F, G) and they move up and down alphabetically on the staff.

G A B C D E F G A B C D E F G A B C D E F

How To Remember The Notes:

Notes On The Lines · **Notes in The Spaces**

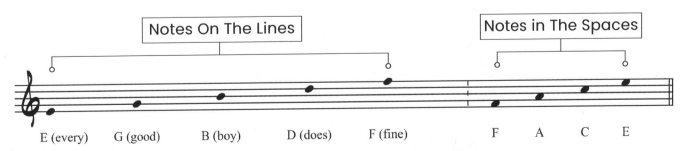

E (every)   G (good)   B (boy)   D (does)   F (fine)   F   A   C   E

UKE LIKE THE PROS.com

B

HOW TO READ TAB

Tablature (TAB) is a form of music reading for Ukulele that has been around for a long time. The TAB staff has 4 lines and each line represents a string on the ukulele. The number represent the fret you play on and are located on the string you play them on.

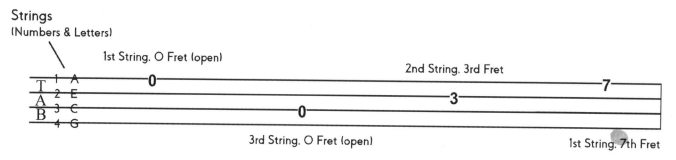

OPEN STRINGS ON THE UKULELE

These are the open string names for a soprano, concert, and tenor ukulele. The only difference between the High G and the Low G is that ukuleles with a Low G have a wider range of notes.

Open String Notes (Ukulele's with High G String):

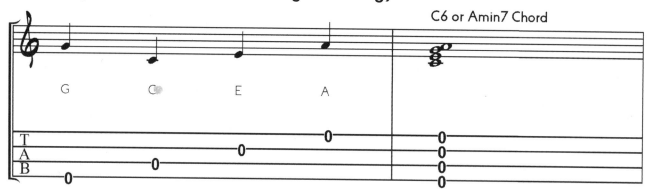

Open String Notes (Ukulele's with Low G String)

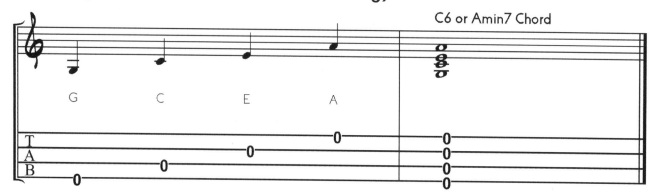

NOTES ON THE UKULELE NECK

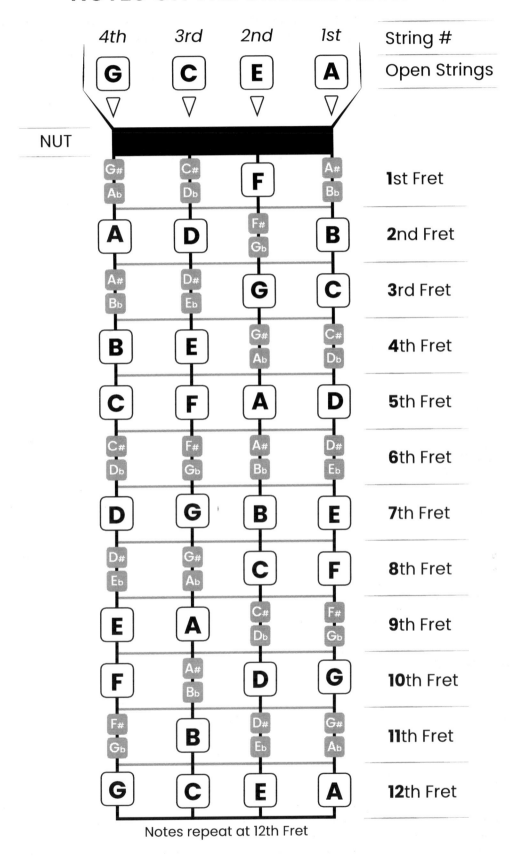

MUSIC SYMBOLS TO KNOW

A variety of symbols, articulations, repeats, hammer on's, pull off's, bends and slides.

Fermata:
Hold note

Staccato:
Play note short

Accent:
Play note loud

Accented Staccato:
Play note
loud + short

Vibrato
Rapid "shaking"
of note

Arpeggiated Chord:
Play the notes in fast
succession from low
to high strings

Grace Note:
Fast embellishment
note played before
the main note

Mute:
"Muffle" sound of
strings either with
left or right hand

Down Stroke:
Pick string(s) with a
downward motion

Up Stroke:
Pick string(s) with
an upward motion

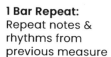

Tie:
Play first note but
do not play second
note that it is tied to

Ledger Lines:
Extend the staff
higher or lower.

Slash Notation:
Repeat notes & rhythms
from previous measure

1 Bar Repeat:
Repeat notes &
rhythms from
previous measure

2 Bar Repeat:
Repeat notes & rhythms
from previous 2 measures

Repeat Sign: (Beginning)	**Repeat Sign:** (End)	**1st Ending:** Play this part the first time only	**2nd Ending:** Play this part the second time

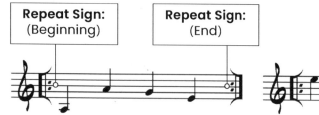
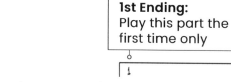
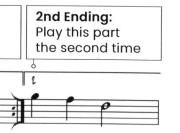
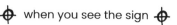

(D.C. AL FINE) — *D.C.* (da capo) means go to the beginning of the tune and stop when you get to *Fine*

(D.C. AL CODA) — *D.C.* means go to the beginning of the tune and jump to *Coda* ⊕ when you see the sign ⊕

(D.S. AL FINE) — *D.S.* (dal segno) means go to the *Sign* 𝄋 and stop when you get to *Fine*

(D.S. AL CODA) — *D.S.* means go to the *Sign* 𝄋 And Jump to the *Coda* ⊕ when you see ⊕

SIM... — Play the same rhythm, strum pattern, or picking pattern as the previous measure

ETC... — Continue the same rhythm, strum pattern, or picking pattern as the previous measure

UKE LIKE THE PROS.com

E

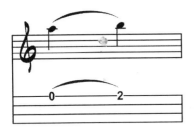

Hammer On:
Pick first note then hammer on
to the next note without picking it.

Pull Off:
Pick first note then pull off to
the next note without picking it.

Hammer On & Pull Off:
Pick first note, hammer on to the
next note, and pull off to the last
note all in one motion.

1/2 Step Bend:
Bend the first note
a 1/2 step or 1 fret.

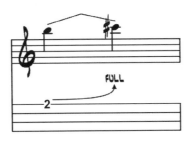

Whole Step Bend:
Bend the first note a whole
step or 2 frets.

Step & 1/2 Bend:
Bend the first note
1 1/2 steps or 3 frets

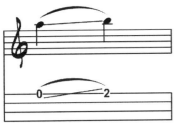

Forward Slide:
Pick first note and slide
up to higher note.

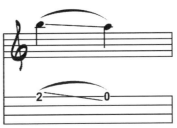

Backward Slide:
Pick first note and
slide back to lower note.

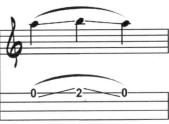

Forward/Backward Slide:
Pick first note, slide up to
next note and then slide back.

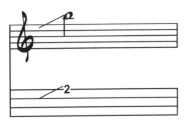

Slide Into Note:
Slide from 2-3 frets below note

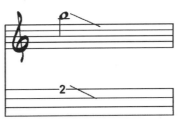

Slide Off Note:
Slide off 2-5 frets after note

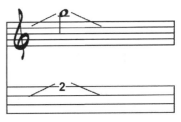

**Slide Into Note
then Slide Off Note**

CHORD CHART

These are some of the most widely used chords in all of music. Although there are more chords than what is listed, these chords represent the most widely used shapes.

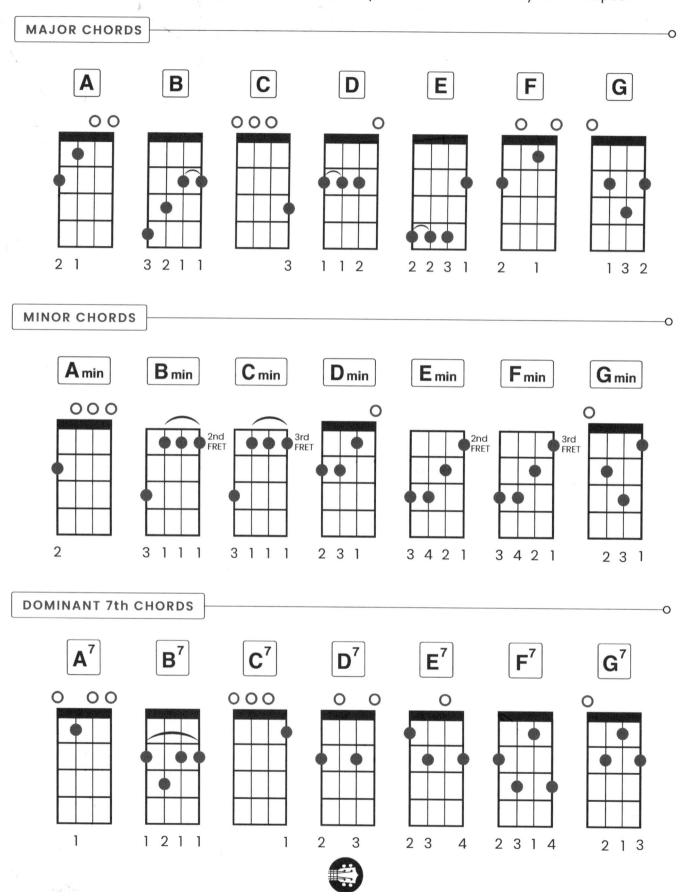

UKE LIKE THE PROS.com

MAJOR 7th CHORDS

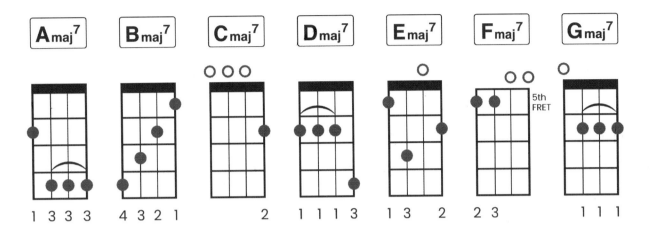

MINOR 7th CHORDS

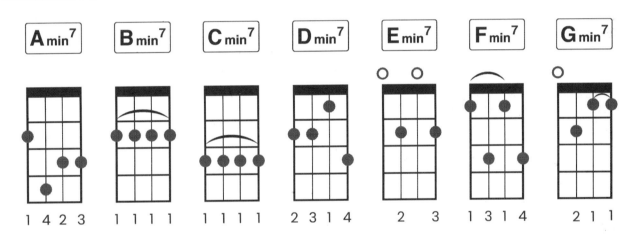

SUS + ADD CHORDS

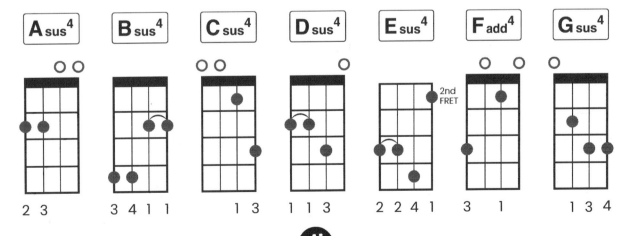

H

Simple Rhythms

The 4 main rhythms in this lesson are whole notes, half notes, quarter notes, and eighth notes.

Strum Technique #1

This lesson uses the "G" and "C" chords. The rhythm uses quarter notes, eighth notes, and half notes played using a Down, Down-Up, Down pattern.

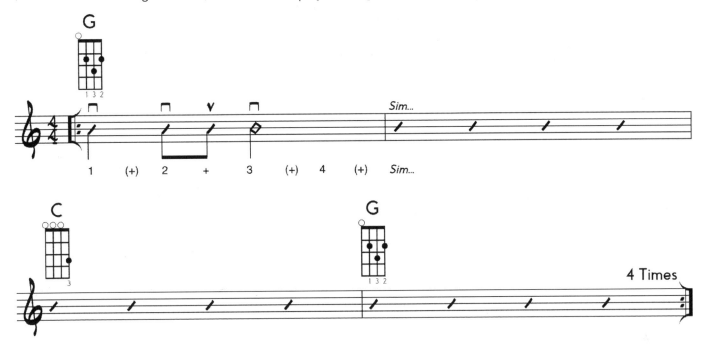

Strum Technique #2

This lesson uses the "G", "C", and "D" chords. The rhythm uses quarter notes and eighth notes played using a Down, Down-Up, Down, Down pattern.

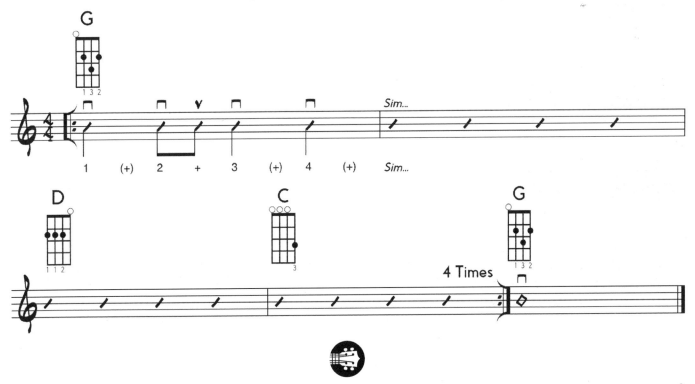

Strum Technique #3

This lesson uses the "Amin", "C" and "G" chords. The rhythm uses quarter notes and eighth notes using a Down, Down, Down-Up, Down-Up pattern.

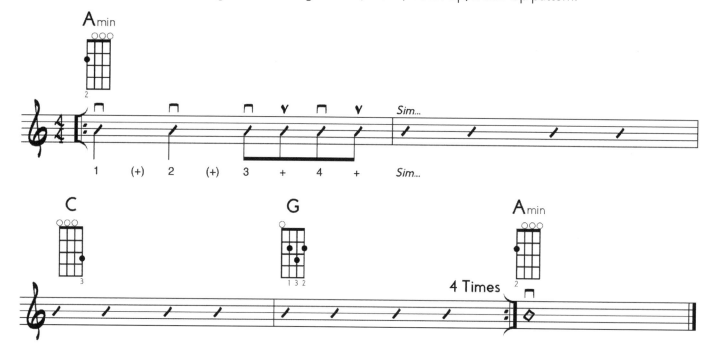

Strum Technique #4

This lesson uses the "C", "F" and "G" chords. The rhythm uses quarter notes and eighth notes using a Down, Down-Up, Down, Down-Up pattern.

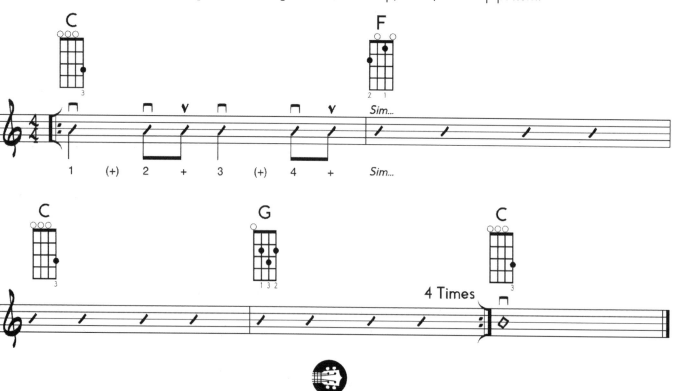

Stum Technique #5

This lesson uses the "Emin", "C", "G", and "D" chords. The rhythm uses quarter notes and eighth notes played in a Down, Down-Up, Down-Up, Down-Up pattern.

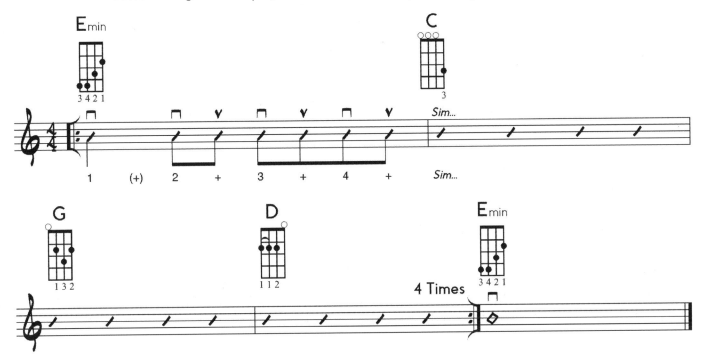

Stum Technique #6

This lesson uses the "A7", "D7" and "E7" chords. The rhythm uses quarter notes and eighth notes with a tie. The tie means to strum on the "+" of beat "2" but don't play on beat "3". The pattern is Down, Down-Up, Up-Down-Up.

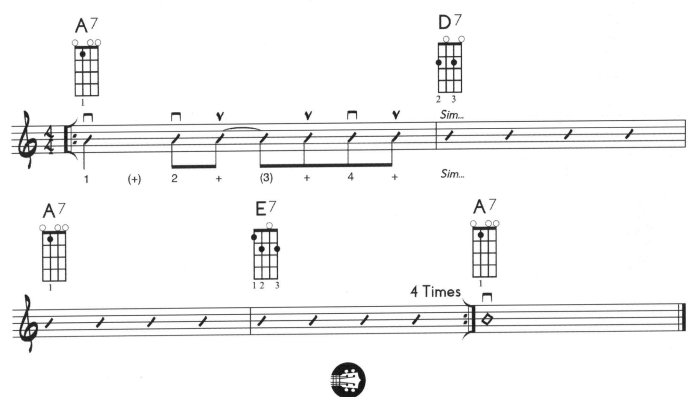

Shine On

(in the style of Let it Be)

This is one of the most important chord progression you will ever learn, it is used in hundreds of songs. The strum pattern uses quarter notes, eighth notes and sixteenth notes.

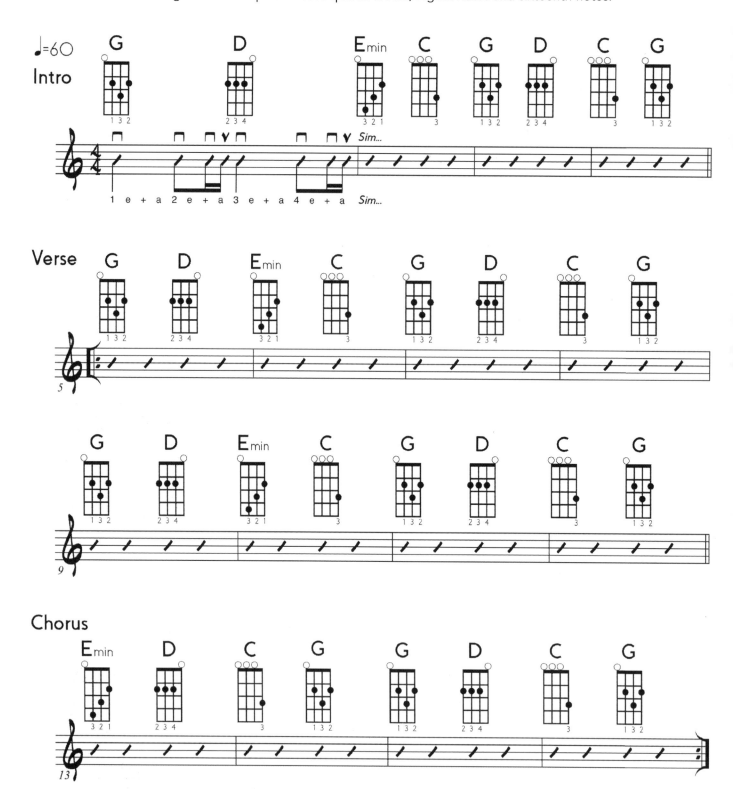

5

Blues Shuffle in A

This blues shuffle works on going between 7th chords and 6th chords. It uses the typical
I (A7), IV (D7), and V (E7) chords and has a 'cool' turnaround in measures 11-12.

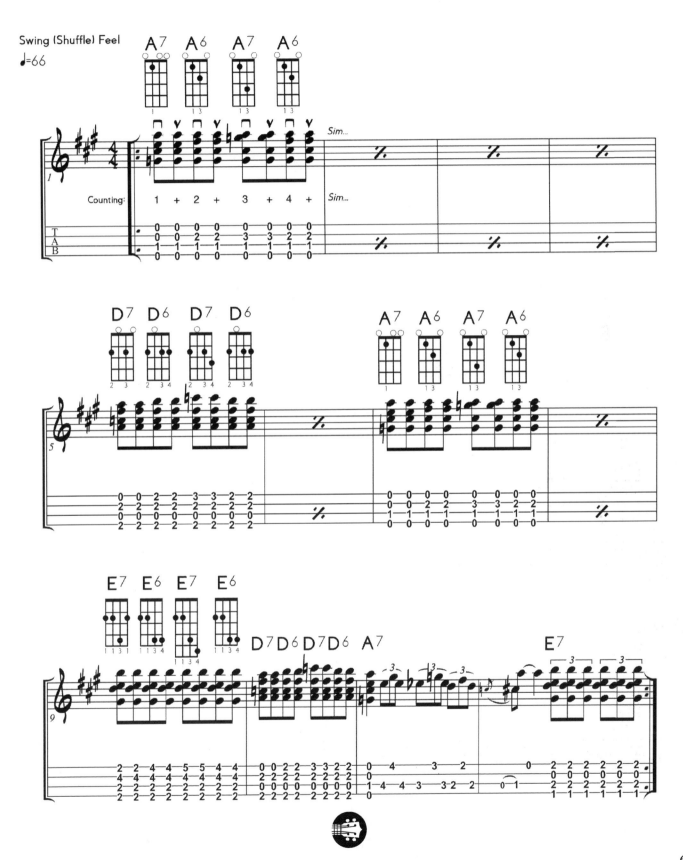

6

Fingerpicking

In this lesson you'll learn the basics of fingerpicking using the P (thumb), i (index) and m (middle) fingers to open up this new world to you. The chords are the same chords you'll see in Brown Eyed Girl, G, C, and D.

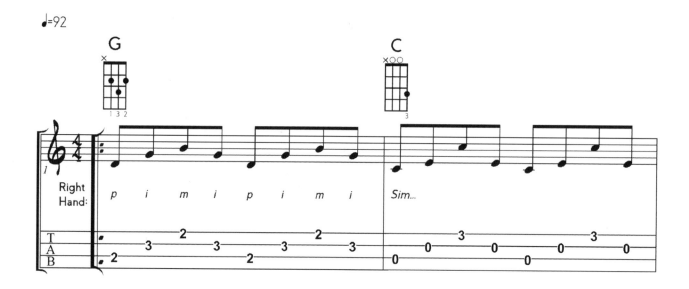

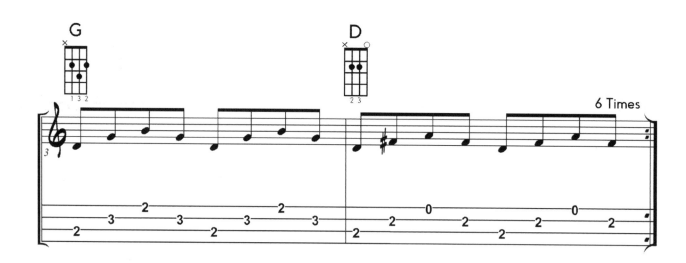

Heaven's Gate

(In the style of Knockin' On Heavens Door)

This song introduces the "Amin" chord. It also incorporates the "G", "C", and "D" chords along with a 1/16 note strum pattern. Feel free to simplfy the rhythm until you get the chords memorized and can change chords while staying on the beat.

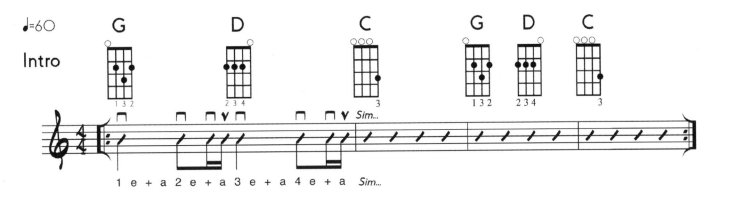

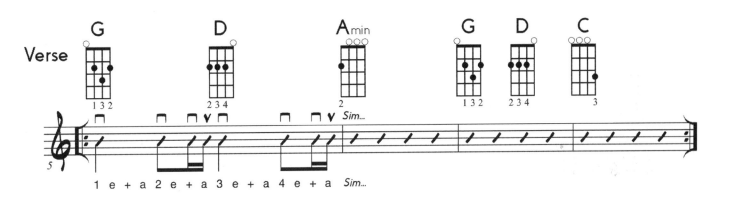

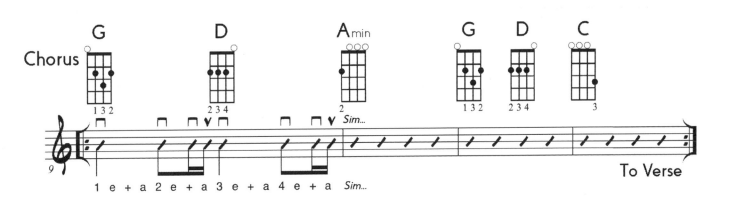

8

My Baby

(In the style of Brown Eyed Girl)

This lesson uses the "granddaddy" strum pattern and once mastered can be used to play songs in any style. It may take a little time to master but once you get it, it will open up the 'secret' to many songs.

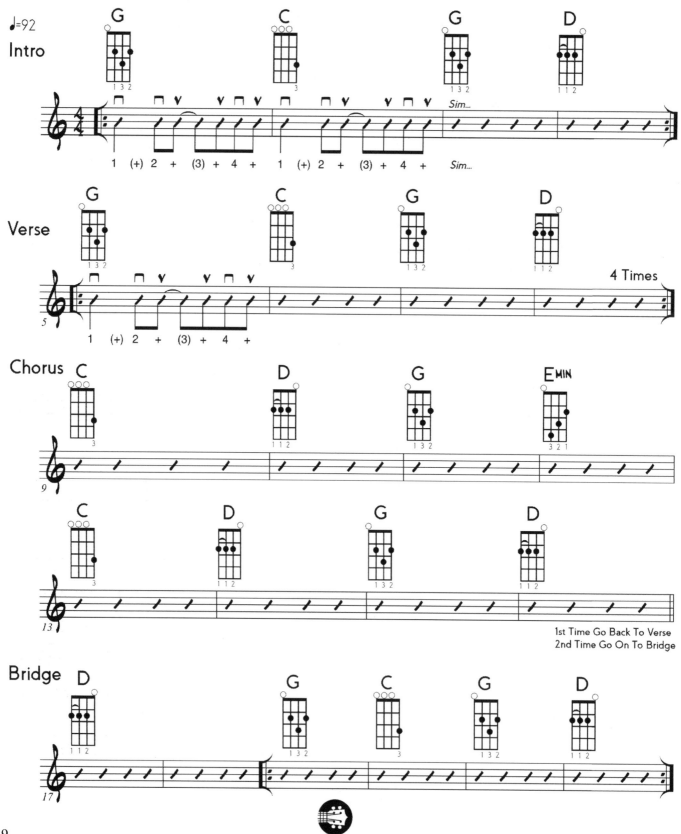

Chuck Berry Rhythm

(In the style of Johnny B. Goode rhythm)

Chuck Berry is known as the Godfather of Rock and Roll. In the early 1950's Chuck Berry took the Blues, sped it up, played with a straight even feel and added fun lyrics and helped create the sound of Rock and Roll. Here we will focus on the rhythm that changed the course of music forever and can be heard on songs such as Johnny B. Goode, Maybelline, and No Particular Place To Go.

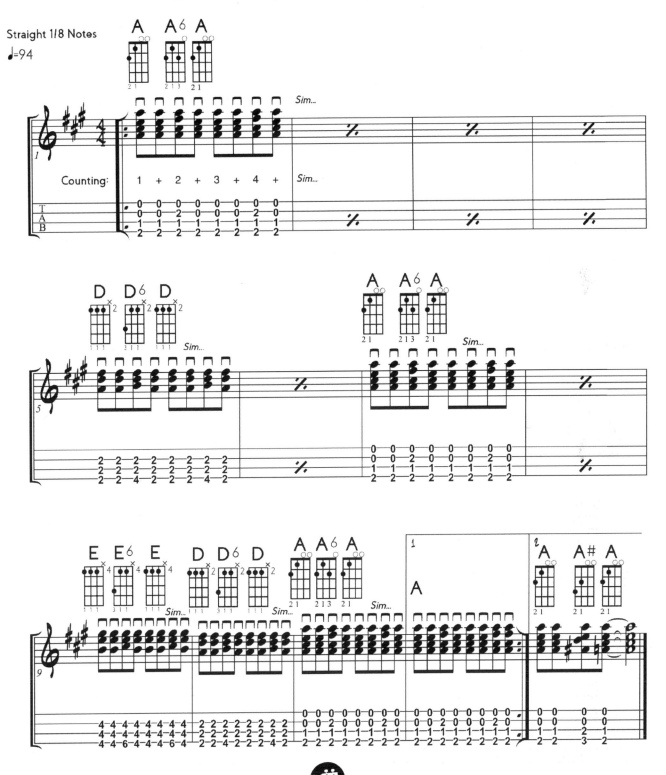

Bayliner

(in the style of Dock of the Bay)

This strum pattern is similar to other songs you learned except that on beat "2" you use a "muted" strum. To get the "muted" sound, place the palm of your strumming hand on the strings right before you strum.

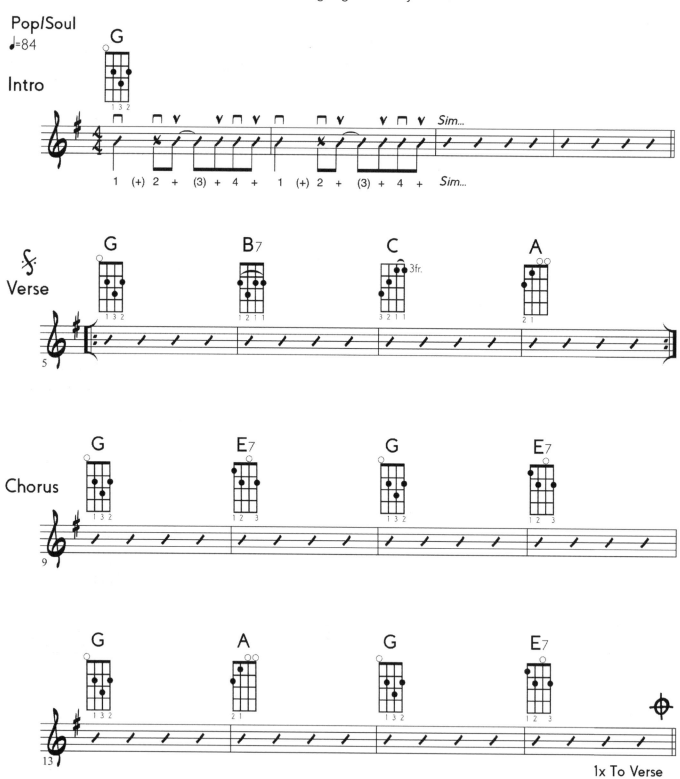

1x To Verse
2x To Bridge

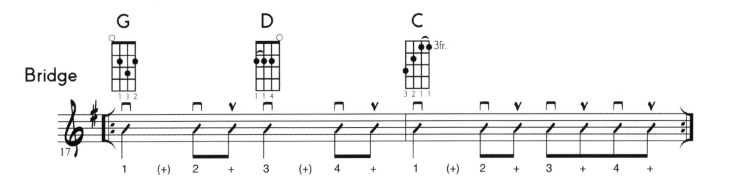

Bridge

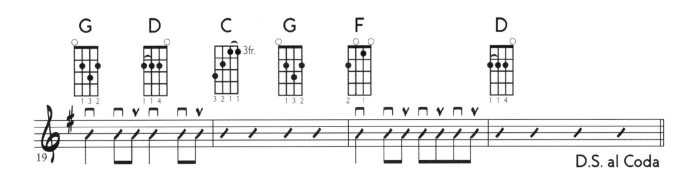

D.S. al Coda

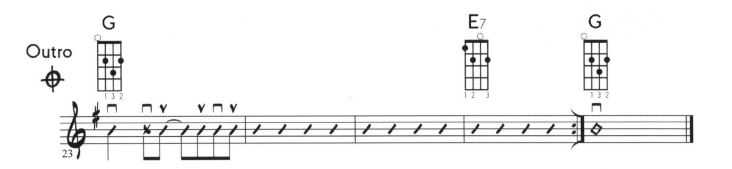

Outro

Muchas Gracias

(in the style of La Bamba)

This strum pattern uses a mute (X) on beat 4 and and a tie on the "+" of 4.
Notice how the "G" chord is "anticipated" because it comes in on the "+" of
4 as opposed to beat 1 on the next measure.

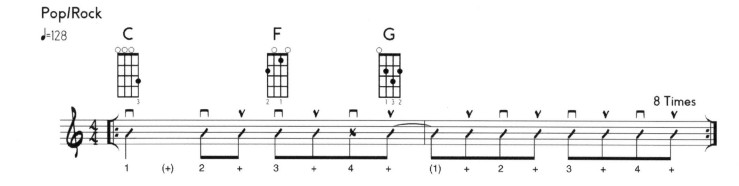

"Let's not go to the grave with the music inside of us"

- Bob Proctor -

"Music is part of my DNA and if I don't get the things I come up with out of my head, I'm unable to function.

- Prince -

Left Hand Man

(in the style of Riptide)

Although this song only uses 4 chords - Amin, G, C, & F, it uses a contemporary
strum pattern with a tie between beats 1 & 2 and 3 & 4.

Hawaiian

♩=100

Intro

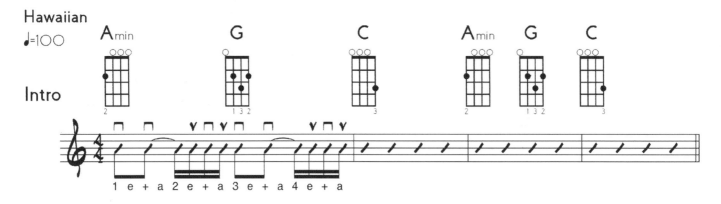

Verse

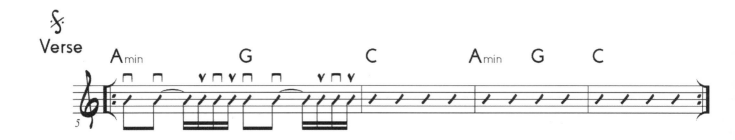

Pre-Chorus

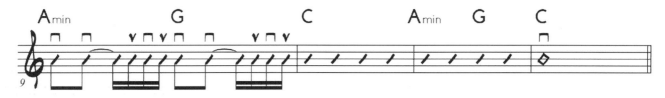

Chorus

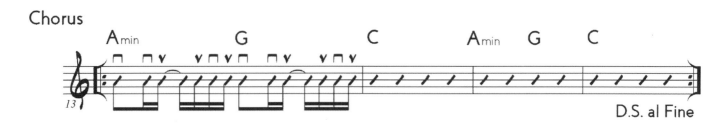

D.S. al Fine

Bridge

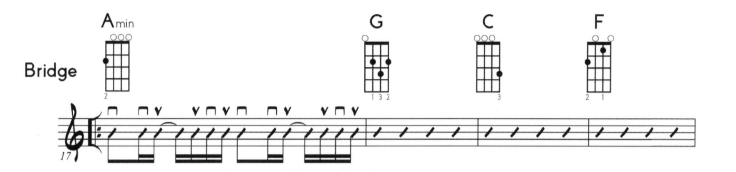

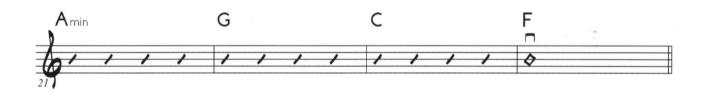

Chorus

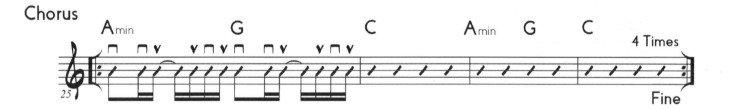

Minor Pentatonic & Blues Scale

The minor pentatonic and the blues scales are the most widely used scales for all styles of music, especially blues, rock, funk, and jazz. It is very important to memorize these scales using the proper fingerings. These scales are used regularly when improvising or soloing.

D Minor Pentatonic Scale

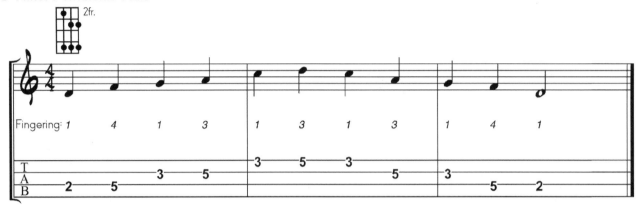

D Blues Scale

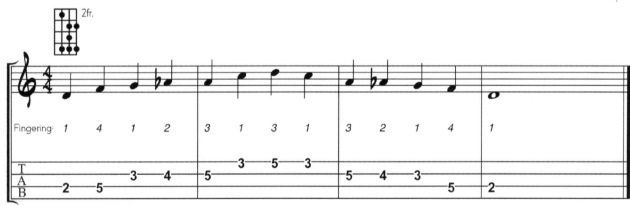

Major Scales

The Major scales is one of the most widely used scales for all styles of music, especially rock, blues, country, and pop. It is very important to memorize these scales using the proper fingerings. These scales are used regularly when creating melodies or soloing.

D Major Scale

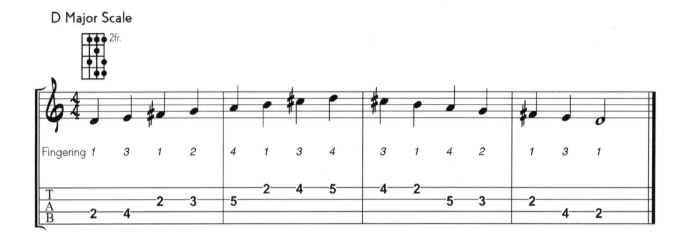

D Major Scale (One String)

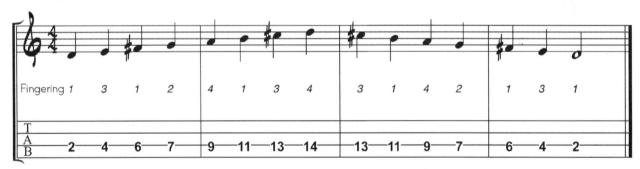

Natural Minor & Harmonic Minor Scales

The Natural Minor scale is very similar to the Minor Pentatonic but adds a few extra notes. It is a really cool and important scale that helps give your solos and melodies a darker or 'sad' feel. The Harmonic Minor is an exotic scale that has a unique sound almost like a Middle Eastern quality to it.

D Natural Minor Scale (Aeolian)

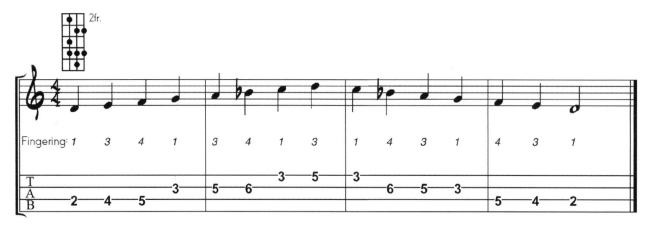

D Harmonic Minor Scale

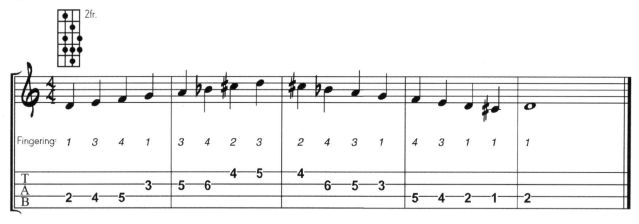

Whole Tone Scale

This cool lesson focuses on the Whole Tone which is a scale entirely made up of Whole Steps. This scale originally gained popularity during the Impressionism Era during the late 1800's and was used predominantly by composers such as Claude Debussy and Maurice Ravel.

D Whole Tone Scale

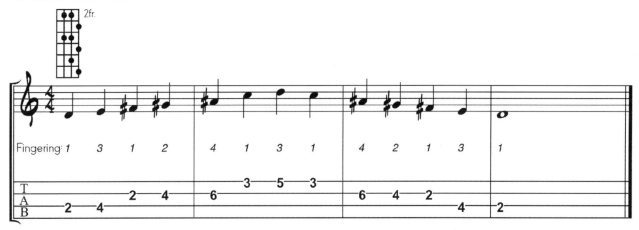

D Whole Tone Scale (One String)

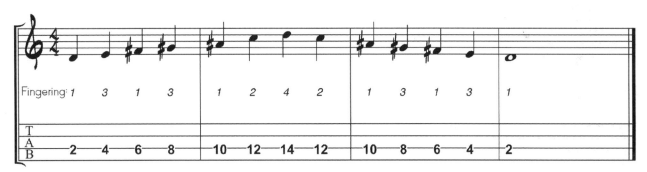

I Won't Hesitate

(in the style of I'm Yours)

This fun island feeling progression by Jason Mraz is a must know for any ukulele player. You'll learn a few new chords on and a funky muted strum pattern.

Pop/Funk

♩=150

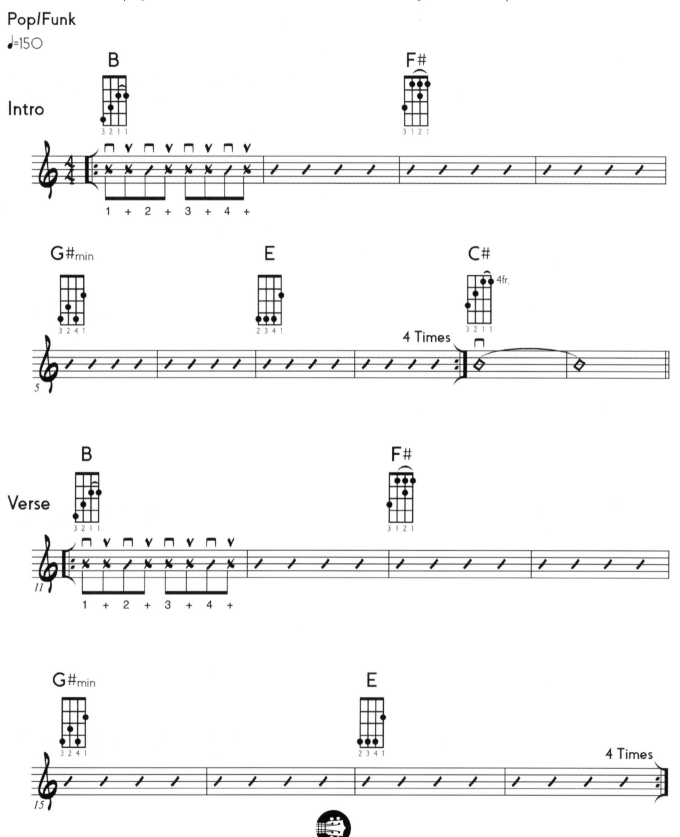

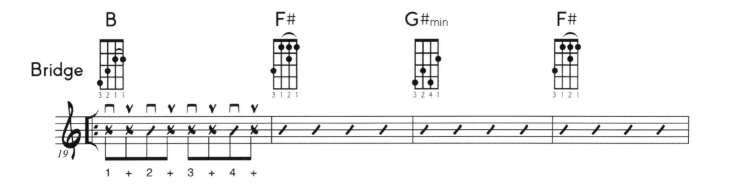

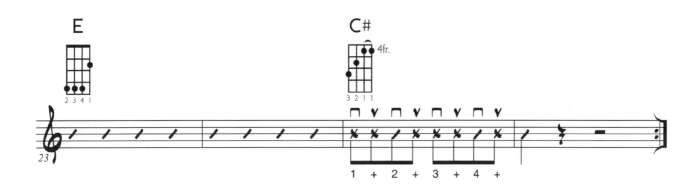

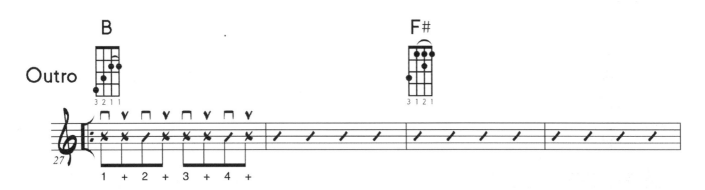

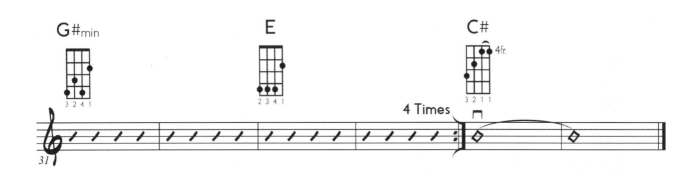

Lemon Drops

(In the style of Somewhere Over The Rainbow)

This is one of the most important chord progressions that you need to know on the ukulele. The strum pattern uses sixteenth notes with a mute (x) on beat 2 and 4.

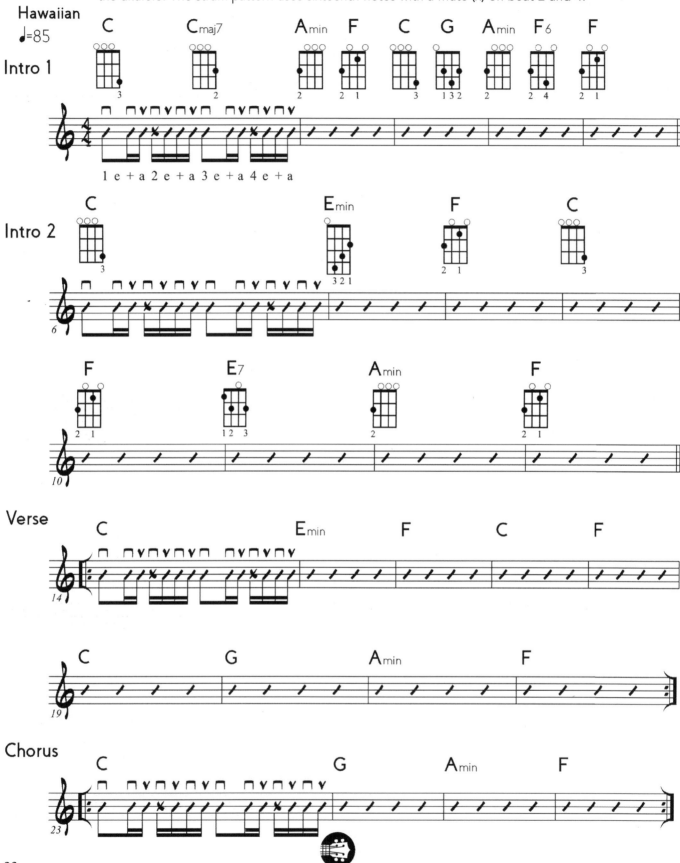

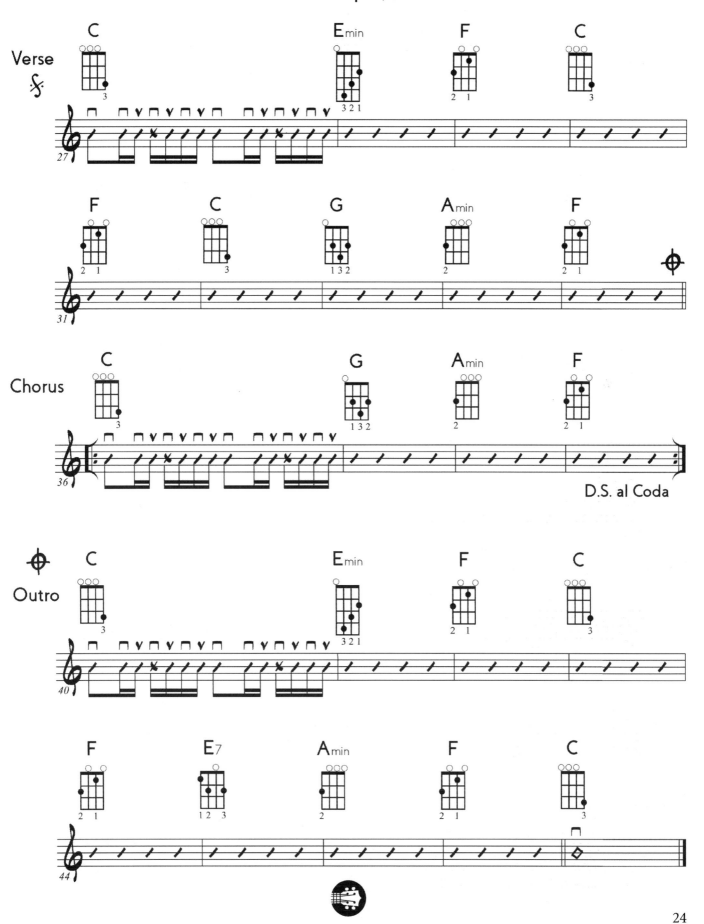

Yellow Canary's

(in the style of Three Little Birds)

This classic progression has a Reggae feel and although it doesn't have alot of chord changes it is important to lock in the 'up stroke' rhythms with the beat.

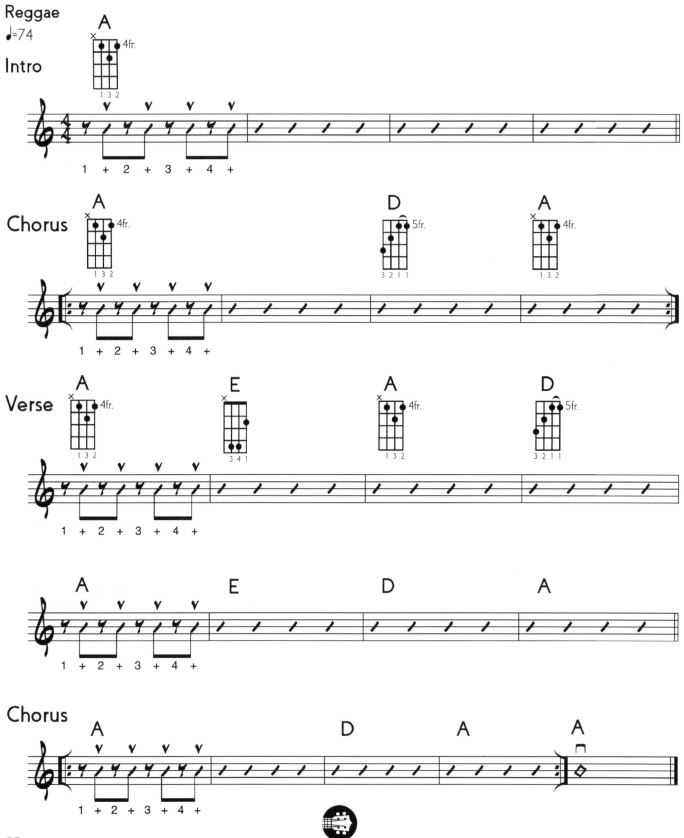

© Uke Like The Pros 2018

Blues Rasgueado

Amaze your friends with the rasgueado technique taken from the world of Flamenco guitar.
We'll keep the chords simply with a standard Blues progresssions but will use a 'rasgueado'
strumming pattern. This one will push your ability but well worth the reward.

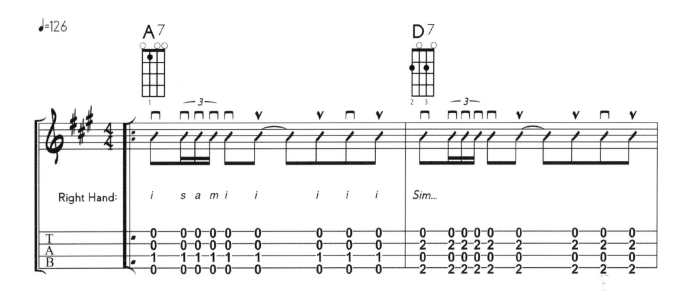

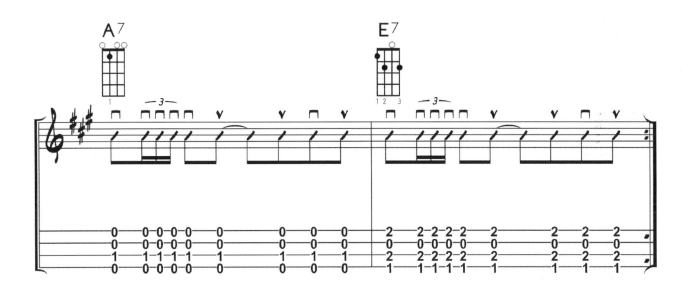

Triplet Strum Pattern Blues

We'll be exploring a strum technique that Jake Shimabukuro uses to dazzle his audiences. The triplet strum pattern can take some time to learn but once mastered you will be able to strum the strings with your 1st finger and your thumb faster then you can with a pick. Also realize that there are many different fingerings that you will see and hear people using hear people using for this triplet pattern.

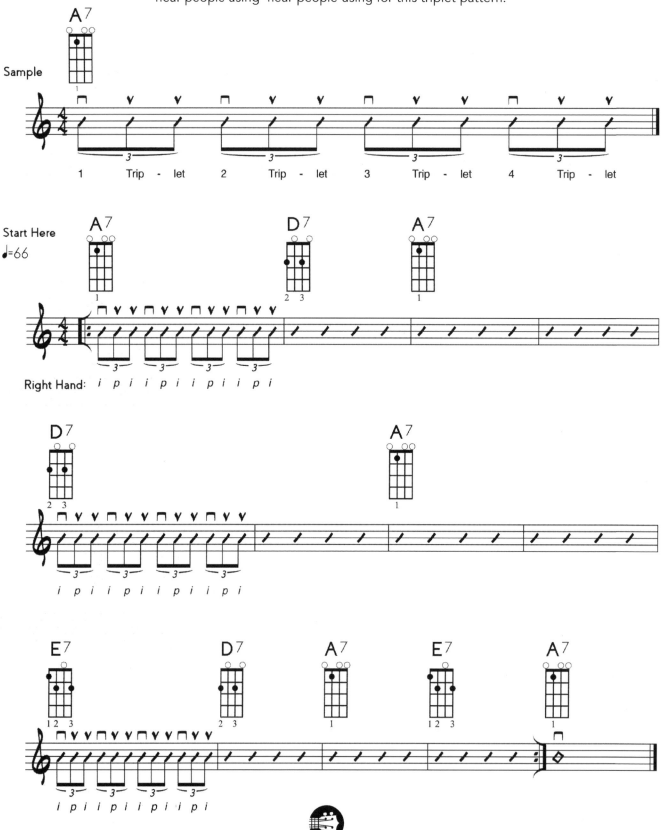

© Uke Like The Pros 2018

Stormy Monday Blues

Written and recorded by T-Bone Walker in 1948 this tune helped encouraged B.B. King to play electric guitar. This 12 bar blues takes the 3 basic blues chords and blows them out of the water with the use of 9th chords, half step sides, walk ups, and a 12/8 feel.

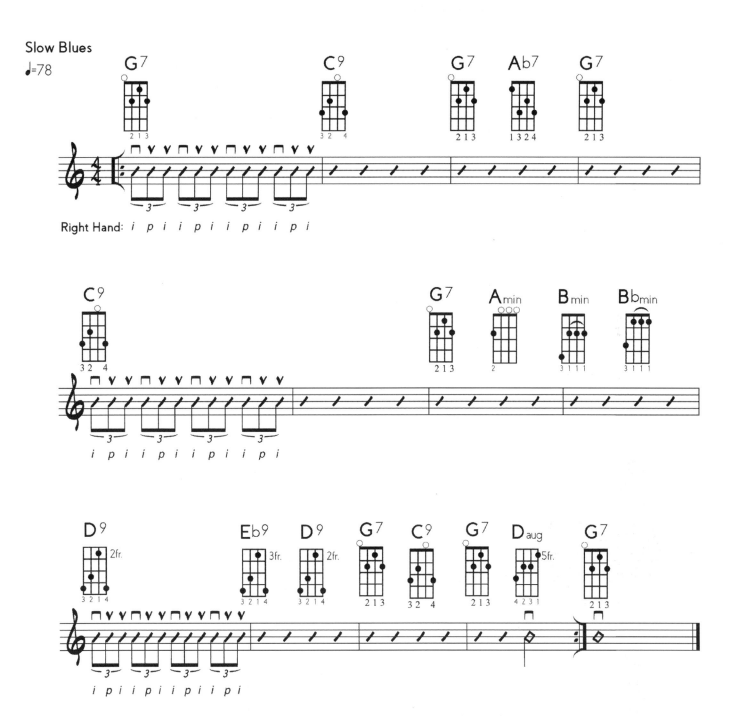

Jazz Blues in Bb

In this lesson we will explore the Jazz Blues. This progression uses 7th chords, 9th chords, minor 7th chords, and a quick change to add 'grease' to the Blues. You will also learn how to use staccato and accented notes to make your strum pattern really 'swing.

Jazz Blues

♩=128

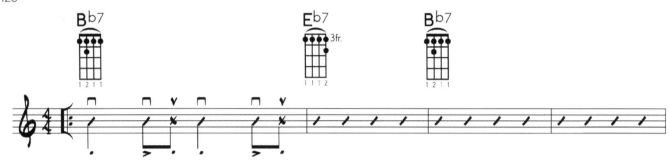

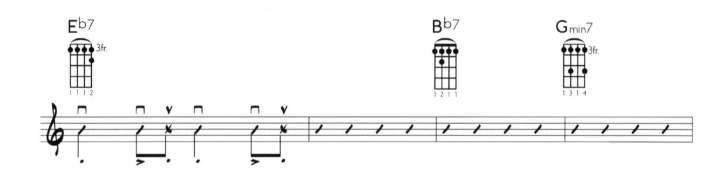

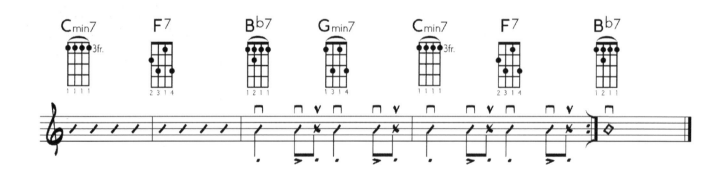

Jazz Blues in Bb

(Fancy Version)

In this lesson we will explore the Jazz Blues. This progression uses 7th chords, 9th chords, minor 7th chords, and a quick change to add 'grease' to the Blues. You will also learn how to use staccato and accented notes to make your strum pattern really 'swing'.

Jazz Blues

About the Author

Terry Carter is a San Diego-based ukulele player, surfer, educator, and creator of Uke Like The Pros. Terry has worked with Weezer, Josh Groban, Robbie Krieger (The Doors), 2 time Grammy winner composer Christopher Tin (*Calling All Dawns*), and the Los Angeles Philharmonic. Terry has written and produced tracks for commercials (Puma) and various television shows, including *Scorpion* (CBS), *Pit Bulls & Parolees* (Animal Planet), *Trippin' and Wildboyz* and *The Real World* (MTV). Terry received a Masters of Music in Studio/Jazz Guitar Performance from University of Southern California and a Bachelor of Music from San Diego State University, with an emphasis in Jazz Studies and Music Education.

Other books from Uke Like The Pros

Ukulele Beginning Music Reading

Music reading is the most important thing you can do as a musician. Not being able to read music is the single biggest factor that will hold your playing back. Once you learn how to read music, not only will you be able to read melodic lines, you will also be able to play chords and strum better than you ever have before. Free yourself from having to read TAB. No prior knowledge or ability of music reading is necessary to succeed in this course. I will start at the very beginning and show you everything you need to know to become a music reading master.

Available on:

Want to play better faster?

Join the growing community at www.UkeLikeThePros.com and get instant access to step-by-step video lessons, courses and improve your playing at a faster rate.

Made in the USA
San Bernardino, CA
08 September 2018